Contents

Unit 1	Mixed-Up Magic	2
	Rhyming words	4
	Writing sentences	5
Unit 2	Fireworks	6
	Sounds around us	8
	The alphabet	8
Unit 3	The Tale of Custard the Dragon	10
	Vowels and consonants	12
	Naming words	13
Unit 4	Paddington	14
	Using reference books	16
	Alphabetical order (first letter)	17
Unit 5	Meet the Smiths	18
	Making a book	19
	Making an index	20
	Alphabetical order (second letter)	20
Unit 6	All the Fun of the Fair	22
	Reading beyond the lines	24
	Describing words	25
Unit 7	What's Cooking?	26
	a or an	27
	Doing words	28
	Alphabetical order (third letter)	28
Unit 8	Words and Meanings	30
	Context	31
	Fill in the Blanks	31
	Days of the Week	31
Unit 9	Checkpoint 1	32
		34
	.swers	35
		36
	ieze	37
Unit 11	Winter Pictures	38
	Making a poem	38
	Describing words	40
Unit 12	Using Books	41
	Book titles	41
	Choosing books	42
	a or an	42
Unit 13	The Boy from Brazil	45
	Limericks	45
	Word pairs	46
	Kim's Game	47
Unit 14	Checkpoint 2	49
Unit 15	Mrs Pepperpot at the Airport	51
	Nouns and verbs	52
	Describing words	52
	Missing words	53
Unit 16	First and Last	54
	Cardinal and ordinal numbers	54
	Picture interpretation	56
	Simple map interpretation	57
Unit 17	Can Machines Think?	58
	Your senses	59
	Describing words	60
	Singular and plural nouns	61
Unit 18	Checkpoint 3	62

UNIT 1

Mixed-Up Magic

Mirium was a witch.

One day she read a notice about a Dog Show. She wanted to go, so, before you could say "Mixed-Up Magic", she was among the dogs, chatting away and having a lovely time.

Just then a policeman came up to her.

"Pardon me, lady," he said. "If you don't have a dog, you can't stay here. You'll have to sit in the stands."

Mirium didn't want to sit in the stands so she said, "I do have a dog."

"Where is it?" asked the policeman.

"Right here in my big, black bag," said Mirium.

"May I see your dog, please?" the policeman asked.

"Oh no," said Mirium, "he's asleep. I don't want to wake him."

All this time Mirium was trying to think of the magic words to make a dog.

"I would still like to see your dog," said the policeman.

Mirium closed her eyes. She said the first magic words that came into her head.

"Abbra-cadabbra, fly like an arrow."
She opened her bag. There was a sparrow.

From *Mixed-Up Magic*
by Wayne Carley and John McInnes

 A. Write answers to these questions.

1. Who are the two people in the story?
2. Where did people without dogs sit?
3. Mirium said, "I do have a dog."
   Was she telling the truth?
4. Where did she say the dog was?
5. Do you think the policeman believed her?
6. Mirium didn't want to open her bag. Why?
7. What reason did she give for not opening her bag?
8. What were the magic words Mirium said?
9. How do you think Mirium felt when she saw a sparrow? Choose from: big, embarrassed, happy.

 B. Words

Mirium said some magic words.
What are words?

1 They can be heard.   When?
2 They can be seen.   Where?
3 They can be spoken. How?
4 They can be thought. Why?

 **C. Rhyming words**

1 Mirium said:
   "Abbra-cadabbra, fly like an arrow."
   She opened her bag. There was a sparrow.

   Arrow and **sparrow** are rhyming words. So are **witch** and **ditch**, **dog** and **frog**, **fly** and **pie**.

   Find rhyming words to go with these words.

   hoot   stand   boat

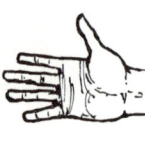

 2 Read the words in the box.

fly	bark	heap	rat
away	dish	grand	hair
high	where	shark	sleep
pat	wish	stay	and

Now write 2 words from this box to rhyme with

(a) cat *rat pat*   (e) hand
(b) lark   (f) deep
(c) fish   (g) my
(d) play   (h) hare.

D. Sentences

> **Yesterday morning I met a witch.**

The words in the box are a sentence.
A sentence is made up of words
which together make sense.
A sentence begins with a capital letter.
A sentence ends with a full stop.

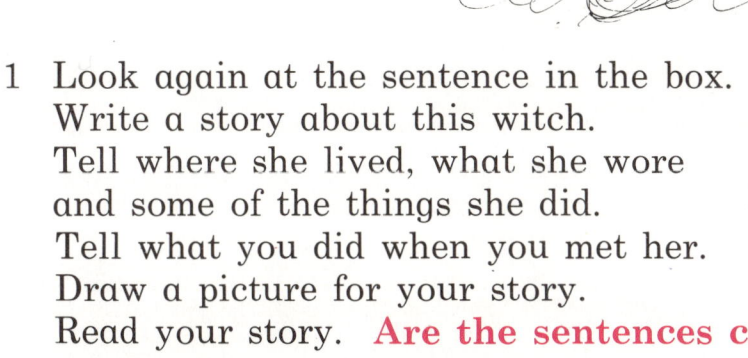

1. Look again at the sentence in the box.
   Write a story about this witch.
   Tell where she lived, what she wore
   and some of the things she did.
   Tell what you did when you met her.
   Draw a picture for your story.
   Read your story. **Are the sentences correct?**

2. Make some magic spells of your own.
   Begin: Abbra-cadabbra …

E. Find out

How many different sorts
of dogs can you name?

F. Extra

In the story of Hansel and Gretel there is a
wicked witch. Make your hands and your face
look like those of a wicked witch.

If you have some musical instruments, make
music for a witch's dance. Dance to it.

UNIT 2

Fireworks

They rise like sudden fiery flowers
  That burst upon the night,
Then fall to earth in burning showers
  Of crimson, blue, and white.

Like buds too wonderful to name,
  Each miracle unfolds,
And catherine-wheels begin to flame
  Like whirling marigolds.

Rockets and Roman candles make
  An orchard of the sky,
Whence magic trees their petals shake
  Upon each gazing eye.

(James Reeves)

Did you like this poem?
Say why you did or didn't.

The Gunpowder Plot

In the year 1605, some men plotted to kill their King. The plotters knew that the King would be coming to the Houses of Parliament on the 5th of November.

That would be the time to kill him.

The plotters hid barrels of gunpowder in the cellars of the Houses of Parliament. Guy Fawkes hid there too. It was his job to set the gunpowder alight and blow up the Houses of Parliament. He did not know, however, that the King had been told about the secret plot.

While Guy Fawkes waited, searchers came to look for him. They found the barrels of gunpowder. They found Guy Fawkes. They took him prisoner and put him in the Tower of London.

Three months later he was executed.

A. Write answers to these questions.

1 What was the date of the Gunpowder Plot?
2 Who was to be killed?
3 Who was to carry out the plot?
4 Was the plot successful?
5 How do you think Guy Fawkes would feel when he was hiding in the cellars? Choose from: comfortable, nervous, kind.
6 Which words mean (a) underground room, (b) put to death, (c) known by only a few people?

B. Sounds

1 Talk with your group and teacher about the sounds you might hear on Bonfire Night. Do you like them? Do you think animals and pets like them?

 2 Listen to the sounds around you. What do you hear now? What sounds might you hear at home, in the street, at the seaside?

 3 Some sounds are pleasant to hear, some are not.

Make two headings in your workbook:

Sounds I like.   Sounds I don't like.

Write at least 5 sounds under each heading. Start with the ones you have been talking about.

C. The Alphabet

An alphabet is a set of letters used to make words. Here are the 26 letters in order.

Small letters

a b c d e f g
h i j k l m n
o p q r s t u
v w x y z

Capital letters

A B C D E F G
H I J K L M N
O P Q R S T U
V W X Y Z

 Write the alphabet twice. Write it once in small letters and once in capital letters.

D. Act the story of Guy Fawkes.

Pretend you are secretly meeting your friends to talk about the plot. What would you say? How would you get the barrels of gunpowder to the cellars?

How would you choose someone to set it alight?

How would you feel if you were Guy Fawkes hiding in the cellar – especially when the searchers arrived?

E. Write a story.

Pretend you are Guy Fawkes. Tell your story up to the time you were taken to the Tower of London.

Check your story by reading it.
Have you written in sentences?
Does each sentence begin with a capital letter?
Does each sentence end with a full stop?

F. Find out.

Find out how people dressed in the year 1605. Draw some pictures showing what people looked like and what they wore at that time.

G. Extra

Fireworks can be very dangerous. Think of some of the ways in which fireworks are dangerous. Make a poster which warns people about the dangers of fireworks.

9

UNIT 3

The Tale of Custard the Dragon

A poet called Ogden Nash wrote a poem about a cowardly dragon who suddenly fought a pirate. Here are three verses of the poem.

Belinda lived in a little white house,
With a little black kitten and a little grey mouse,
And a little yellow dog and a little red wagon,
And a realio, trulio, little pet dragon.

Now the name of the little black kitten was Ink,
And the little grey mouse, she called her Blink,
And the little yellow dog was sharp as
    mustard,
But the dragon was a coward, and she called him
    Custard.

Suddenly, suddenly they heard a nasty sound,
And Mustard growled, and they all looked around.
"Meowch!" cried Ink, and "Ooh!" cried Belinda,
For there was a pirate, climbing in the winda.

                          From *The Face is Familiar*
                                 by Ogden Nash

1. Look at the picture. The dragon and the pirate had a fight. What do you think happened?
2. What other poems or stories about dragons do you know?

A. **Space Adventure**

These six pictures tell part of a story.
Look at them carefully.

At dawn, Diana 2 blasted off.

1. Copy into your workbook the sentence under picture 1.
2. Now write sentences for each of the other pictures.
3. Write more sentences to finish the story. (What happened when the dragon woke up? Did it get the treasure back? Did the treasure bring bad or good luck to the spacemen?)

Read your story. Check that each sentence begins with a capital letter and ends with a full stop.

 B. Spelling

> **Spelling is saying or writing correctly the letters that make a word.**

1. Why do you need to know how to spell?
2. What do you do if you don't know how to spell a word?
3. When you were reading the poem about Custard, did you notice the word "winda"? That is not the correct spelling. What should it be? Why did the poet choose a spelling that was not correct?

C. The Alphabet

The letters a e i o u/A E I O U are called **vowels**.

The other letters of the alphabet are called **consonants**.

Every word in the English language has at least one vowel.

The letter y is sometimes used as a vowel and sometimes as a consonant. In **my** it is used as a vowel, in **yes** it is used as a consonant.

1. Copy into your workbook the words in the box. Draw a line under all the vowels.

car	fly	hamster	rabbit
mouse	elephant	dinosaur	yellow

2. Now write two words with

   (a) one vowel (b) two vowels (c) three vowels.

D. **Nouns**

Naming words are nouns.

1 There is a naming word under each picture. Read the naming words.

2 Tell the names of things in the classroom.

E. **Name the pictures.**

1 Write a name for each picture.

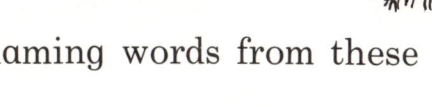

2 Write the naming words from these sentences:
(a) My book is on the desk.
(b) The train stopped at every station.
(c) In my bag I have a pencil, pen, rubber, ruler and book.

F. **Find out.**

What really happened to the pirate in "The Tale of Custard the Dragon"?

UNIT 4

Paddington

The Brown household was unusually quiet and peaceful that afternoon for Paddington had the house to himself. In the morning the postman had brought Jonathan and Judy a surprise invitation to a tea party, and by the same delivery a letter had arrived asking Mrs Brown and Mrs Bird to visit an old aunt who lived on the other side of London.

Even Paddington should have been out, for Mr Brown had given him several books to take back to the Public Library together with a long list of things he wanted looking up in the Reference Department.

From *Paddington at Large*
by Michael Bond

A. Write answers to these questions.

1. In whose house did Paddington live?
2. The house was quiet and peaceful. Why was this?
3. Did Jonathan and Judy know they were going to be asked to a party? How do you know?
4. How do you think Mrs Brown and Mrs Bird would travel to the aunt's house?
5. What is a Public Library?
6. Why do you think Mr Brown had not gone there himself?
7. Are you a member of a Public Library?

 **B. What do they do?**

1. A librarian works in a library.
   What do these people do?

   (a) dentist   (c) policeman   (e) butcher
   (b) hairdresser   (d) miner   (f) doctor

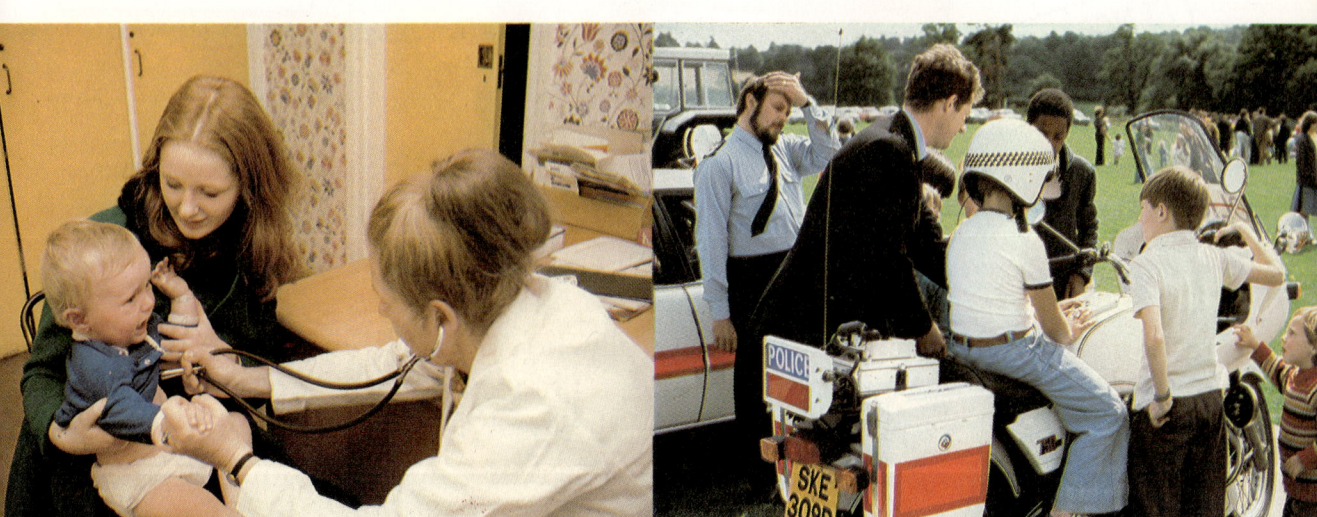

Name other kinds of workers. What do they do?

 2. What kind of work would you like to do when you grow up? Tell about the work and why you want to do it. Begin: *When I grow up*
Draw a picture.

C. Finding out

1 In Units 1, 2 and 3 of *Wordpower*, when this little picture appeared, you had to find out something. What did you do?

2 Paddington used books in the Public Library to find out things.

   Here are some of the books he might have seen.

These are not story books which you read from beginning to end. They are information books which tell about things you are interested in.

Suppose you wanted to find out about the Apollo moon rocket. You would look in *Transport, General Knowledge* and *Space Travel*.

 In which of the books would you find out about

(a) the first motor car?
(b) lions and tigers?
(c) Queen Victoria?

D. Using a dictionary

A dictionary tells you what words mean and how to spell them. The words are arranged in alphabetical order. If you do not know the alphabetical order it is hard to find the word you want.

> **ket**
>
> trees grow so thickly that it is hard to find your way through
>
> **junior**   someone who is younger or less important than others
>
> **junk**   something of no use or value; rubbish. The same word also means a Chinese sailing ship.
>
> **jut**   to stick out
>
> **kaleidoscope**   a toy shaped like a tube, with small pieces of coloured glass which change patterns when you turn the tube round
>
> **kangaroo**   an animal which can jump a long way. It has a pocket for its babies.
>
> **keel**   a heavy piece of wood or metal that goes along the bottom of a boat or ship from one end to the other
>
> **keen**   very interested in something. The same word also means sharp; cutting.
>
> **keep**   to hold on to something and not give it away. The same word also means the strongest, inside part of a castle.
>
> **keeper**   someone who looks after or guards something, like a gamekeeper or a keeper at the zoo
>
> **kennel**   a small house or shelter for a dog
>
> **kerb**   the edge of a pavement
>
> **kernel**   the inside part of a nut that can usually be eaten
>
> **kettle**   a metal container used for boiling water. It has a lid, a handle and a spout.

1 Look carefully at these groups of letters.

Copy the first two letters and then write the one that comes next in the alphabet.

(a) ab – (b) fg –
(c) tu – (d) qr –
(e) BC – (f) IJ –
(g) LM – (h) DE –

2 Now put these groups of letters into alphabetical order.

(a) z p b l r f

(b) K C Q M D Y

E. Extra

1 Ask a friend to hear you say the alphabet.
2 Play a group game of *What is the next letter?*

UNIT 5

Look at the family photo. It shows Mr and Mrs Smith (the grandparents) and their daughter and her husband (Mr and Mrs Black) with their three children, Sally, Norman and Susan, who is kneeling.

 A. Now answer these questions.

1. How many grandchildren of Mr and Mrs Smith are in the picture?
2. What is Norman's surname?
3. How many sisters does Norman have?
4. Who is Sally's grandfather?
5. Who is Mrs Black's mother?
6. How many brothers does Susan have?
7. Who is Norman's father?
8. Who are the daughters of Mr and Mrs Black?
9. Who is Mr and Mrs Smith's grandson?
10. Who is Susan's mother?

 B. Your family

Draw a picture of your family.
Make sure you are in it.
Label everybody in your picture.

C. Making a book

Each person will need:

paints or crayons

a pencil

a sheet of paper about the size of a page of *Wordpower*

Now do 4 things.
1 On the top half of your paper make a picture of yourself.
2 On the bottom half write answers to these questions.

    (a) What is your name? *My name is …*
    (b) What age are you? *I am …*
    (c) Where do you live? *I live …*
    (d) How many brothers and sisters have you? *I have …*
    (e) What are your hobbies? *My hobbies are …*

Check that each sentence begins with a capital letter and ends with a full stop.

3 Take your paper to a collection point. If you were first to finish, put 1 at the bottom of your page. If you were second, put 2, and so on until all the pages have been numbered.

4 Leave them in a safe place until the next section is finished.

Making an index for your book

An index is placed at the end of a book.
It helps you to find information quickly.
It is arranged in alphabetical order.

It will help if you read the instructions before doing the work.

(a) Write on the blackboard the first name of each person in your class or group
(if you are making a group book).

(b) Arrange the first letters of these names in alphabetical order.

A
B
J
R
R

(c) With these letters to guide you, write the names on the board again, this time in alphabetical order. If there are 2 names beginning with the same first letter, arrange them by the second letter: **Ross, Ruth**.

If there are 2 names exactly the same, arrange them by the surname: **Mary L., Mary P.**

Ann
Brian
John
Ross
Ruth

(d) Choose someone who writes neatly to copy the names from the board on to a sheet of paper the same size as the picture stories.

(e) Bring out the picture stories. Write the correct page number opposite each name on the list you have made.

← This is the index.

Now complete the book.

1 (a) Arrange the picture stories in order as you would find them in a book: 1, 2, 3 and so on.
   (b) Put the index after the last page.
   (c) Staple all the pages together.

2 Have a competition for a cover design and a name for the book.

3 Put the finished book in the class library. Use the index when you want to read about your friends.

 D. Find out.

Find out from your class or school library the names of five books which have an index. Write down their names.

21

UNIT 6

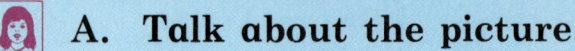 **A. Talk about the picture.**

1 What does the picture show?
2 Which of these words could be used to describe it?

sad	exciting	noisy	busy
gloomy	deep	colourful	silver
slow	bright	empty	

3 What sounds would you hear at a fair?
4 What things would you smell at a fair?
5 What would you do if you went there?

B. Write answers to these questions.

1 Look at the picture. Is it summer or winter?
2 How much does a hot dog cost?
3 Which is higher – the Big Dipper or the Helter Skelter?
4 At which stall did the little girl win the teddy bear?
5 A little boy's balloon has drifted away. How do you think he feels?
6 What is the prize for the Bingo winner?
7 What is the fortune-teller's name?
8 Which would you like better – a ride on the dodgems or a ride on the moon rocket? Why?

C. Notices

1 Look at these notices.
   (a) Do you think the candyfloss is free?
   (b) Do you think that every person who goes to the goldfish stall will get a goldfish?
   (c) What is the meaning of *Have your hand read*?
   (d) What is the meaning of *Queue here*?
   (e) Why do you think you have to queue for the Big Dipper?
   (f) Two of these notices ask you to obey an order. Which two?

2 Answer these questions.
   (a) Where would you see these notices?
   (b) What would you do if you got lost (i) at a fair, (ii) in a town?

E. Words which describe

1 Read these words:

Write in your workbook the words from the left-hand circle and beside each word write a suitable noun from the right-hand circle.

Begin like this: *busy fairground*

2 Read these describing words:

lucky   big   delicious   loud   coloured

Write these sentences, putting a describing word from the box in each space.

(a) Tom won a _____ teddy bear.
(b) A man was selling _____ balloons.
(c) The merry-go-round had _____ music.
(d) Mary's ticket had a _____ number.
(e) There was a _____ smell of hot dogs.

F. Write a story.

Describe a visit to a fair. Tell where it was, what you did, what you ate and what you won. Tell what you enjoyed most.
The story may be real or imaginary.

UNIT 7

What's Cooking?

Granny's big kitchen table looked just like a shop, there were so many things on it. There were jars and bottles and packets, full of currants and sultanas and raisins and ginger and candied peel, and a big heap of suet on a board, and a big heap of brown sugar on a plate. There were apples and oranges and lemons, and even some big clean carrots!

There was a big brown bowl that had a big, big wooden spoon in it, and on the draining board were lots of white basins.

Can you guess? My sister couldn't. She didn't know what all the stuff was for, so Granny said, "We are going to make the Family Christmas Puddings."

From *When my Naughty Little Sister was Good* by Dorothy Edwards

A. Write answers to these questions.
1 Why was Granny's kitchen table like a shop?
2 What was Granny going to make?
3 What vegetable is spoken about?
4 What do you think the big brown bowl was for?
5 Why were there lots of white basins?
6 Which word means a kind of fat for cooking?
7 Where would you find a draining board?
8 How could the children help Granny?

B. a or an

1 Do you like making things to eat?
To make a fruit salad you will need

an apple   an orange   a banana

a pear   a peach   a lemon

a small tin of fruit juice.

Say what you would do with these things to make a fruit salad.

2 Look at the list of fruit.
Each fruit has either **a** or **an** before it.
Can you spot when **a** was used and when **an** was used? Were you right? Use **a** before a consonant, **an** before a vowel.

       a pear   **an o**range

3 Put **a** or **an** correctly in the spaces.
Write the sentences.
  (a) I had _____ egg for breakfast.
  (b) It was _____ fried egg.
  (c) The cake was baked in _____ electric oven.
  (d) It was _____ chocolate cake.
  (e) I like _____ packet of crisps at playtime.

C. Verbs

> **Doing words are called verbs.**

Here are some of the things Granny did when she made her puddings.

She **weighed** the sugar.   She **poured** it into bowls.
She **washed** the fruit.   She **cooked** the puddings.
She **stirred** the mixture.

 1 What other things might Granny do?

 2 Write these sentences correctly, putting a different word from the box in each space.

> **whisked   squeezed   sifted   peeled**

(a) She _____ the lemons.
(b) She _____ the eggs.
(c) She _____ the oranges.
(d) She _____ the flour.

D. Alphabetical order

 1 Here are 8 things to eat.

> **pancakes   buns   sponge   gingerbread**
> **spaghetti   jelly   soup   peas**

Write them in alphabetical order. Before you do this, look at the three which begin with the same letter: soup, sponge, spaghetti. Arrange them by the second letter, so s**o**up comes first. The other two words – **sponge** and **spaghetti** – have the same second letter. Arrange them by the third letter, so sp**a**ghetti comes before sp**o**nge.

E. Washing day

The Washing Machine

It goes fwunkety
Then shlunkety
as the washing goes around.

The water spluncheses
Then it shluncheses
as the washing goes around.

As you pick it out it splocheses
Then it flocheses
as the washing goes around.

But at the end it shlopperies
and then it flopperies
and the washing stops going round.

(Jeffrey Davies)

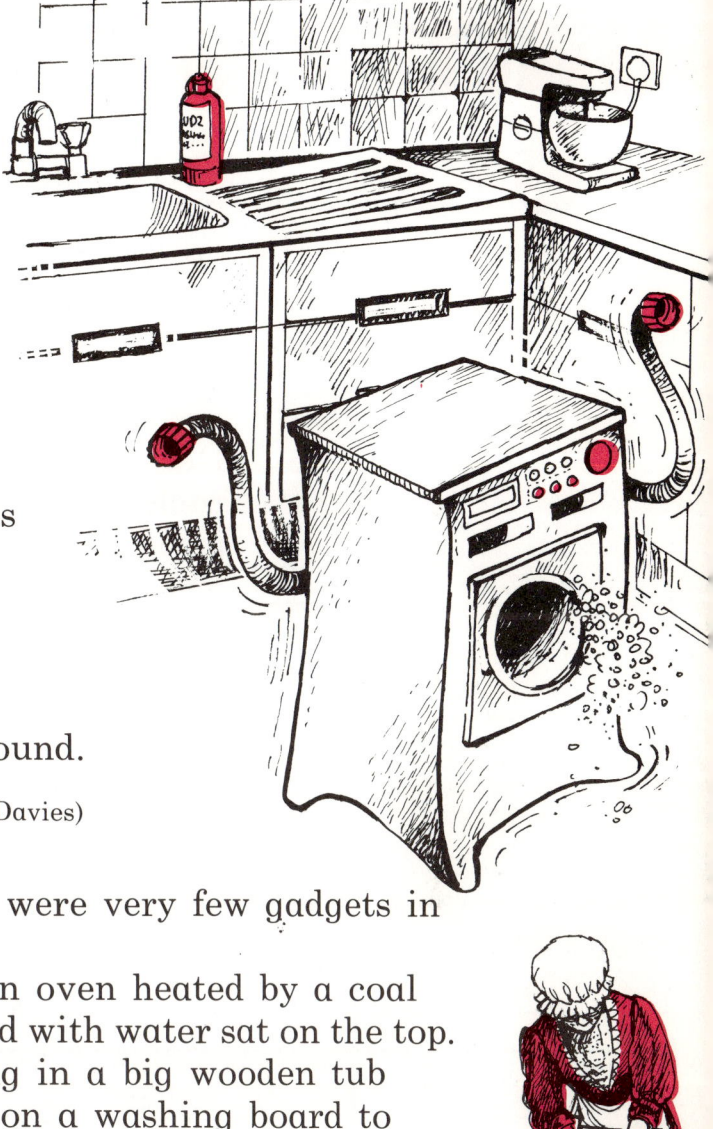

In times gone by, there were very few gadgets in the kitchen.

Baking was done in an oven heated by a coal fire. An iron kettle filled with water sat on the top.

People did the washing in a big wooden tub and rubbed the clothes on a washing board to clean them.

There was no electricity.

Talk about all the gadgets in today's houses. Say how you think people did the work without them.

Write a list of gadgets that now help to make housework easier.

F. Extra

Design a machine which will put away all the shopping when it is brought home. Draw a picture of it and tell how it works.

29

 A. **Meanings**

1 What is the meaning of the red word in each sentence?
(a) Hammer the **post** into the ground.
(b) **Post** the letter before noon.
(c) The boy's **watch** stopped.
(d) What do you **watch** on television?
(e) The girl did not feel **well**.
(f) Is there any water in the **well**?

Did you notice that **post**, **watch** and **well** each had two meanings? You could tell the meanings of these words from the words around them.

2 Look at the pictures.
Read the sentences in the box.
Write the sentences in the order in which the pictures are set out.

(a) **The parcel was light.**	(c) **I woke before it was light.**
(b) **Julie wore a light blue dress.**	(d) **Please light the fire.**

Did you notice that the word **light** had 4 meanings? The words around it helped you to understand.

B. Missing words

Read this story and, as you read, try to think of words to fill the spaces. The words around the spaces will help you to choose the missing word. Copy the story into your workbook when you have chosen the words.

It was midnight. Bill Tomkins was walking down the _____. Suddenly he heard the screech of _____. A car had stopped at the _____ lights. The driver was in such _____ hurry that he drove off again _____ the green light came on. "That _____ how accidents happen," said Bill Tomkins.

C. Days of the week

Here are the 7 days of the week:

Sunday, Monday, Tuesday, Wednesday, Thursday, Friday, Saturday.

1. Say them over to yourself, then cover them and try to write them in order.
Check that they are in the correct order and that the spelling is correct, too. (Remember the capital letter.)
2. The name of a day is missing from each sentence.
Write each sentence and put in the missing word.
(a) Today is _____.
(b) Yesterday was _____.
(c) Tomorrow will be _____.
(d) The day of the week I like best is _____.
(e) The day after tomorrow will be _____.

D. Extra

Draw a picture called **The Accident**. Display the drawings and tell about yours.

UNIT 9

Checkpoint 1

1. Write the 5 vowels in small letters.
   Now write them in capital letters.

2. Write any six consonants.

3. What letter comes next in the alphabet?
   Write the group of three.

   de– kl– st– ij– pq–

   FG– MN– QR– AB– HI–

4. Write in pairs the words that rhyme.

   size   name   soft   lies   wait

   loft   bite   game   late   light

5. Write these animals in alphabetical order.

   lion   panda   kangaroo   tiger   elephant

   camel   giraffe   monkey   bear   deer

6. Write these as correct sentences, putting in capital letters and full stops.

   (a) we saw a film on wednesday

   (b) on tuesday mary had a party

   (c) i hope i shall see you on saturday

7. Write the words below, putting **a** or **an** correctly before each word.

   emu   pen   ostrich   American

   cup   box   island   road

8. Write your name and address.

9. Write today's date.

10 Write all the nouns (naming words) from these sentences.

The small room had a table, two chairs and an old wooden chest. A lamp was lit. It cast a shadow over the wall. John waited.

11 Write all the verbs (doing words) from this sentence.

Mother washed the clothes, dried them, ironed them and aired them.

12 Write all the describing words from these sentences:

(a) The fast car roared along the quiet road.

(b) As it was a sunny morning, the old lady took her little dog for a short walk.

(c) The happy children sledged down the steep hill.

Extra

Look at number 10, above. Write a story telling why John waited. Did someone come? What happened?
Begin. *John waited.*

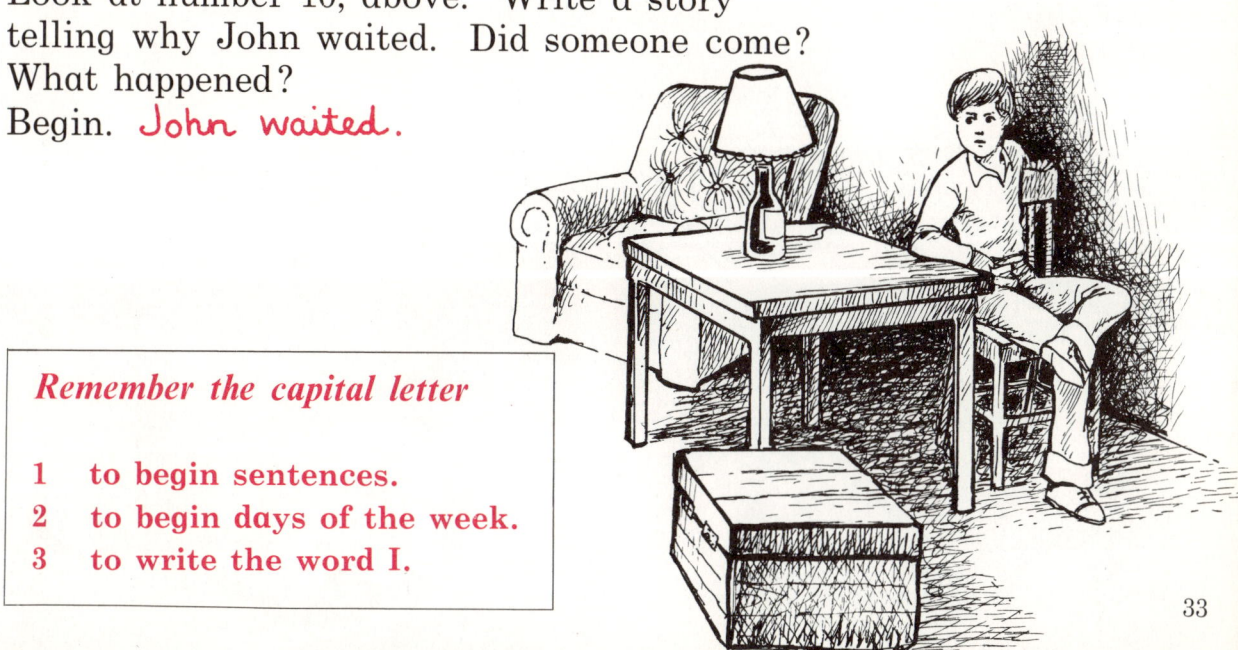

Remember the capital letter

1   to begin sentences.
2   to begin days of the week.
3   to write the word I.

UNIT 10

What is happening in the picture?
Name the vehicles called to help with the fire.
How would each one be called?
Form groups and act out "A Fire".

A. Questions

1 Asking questions is a way of finding out things.
   You might ask:
      How did the fire start?
   The answer might be:
      A chip pan caught fire.
   What other answers can you think of?

   When you write a question, a question mark ?
   is put at the end of the sentence, like this:
      Whose house is on fire?

2 Write answers to these questions.
   Write in sentences. Remember the full stop.
   (a) How many fire-engines are there?
   (b) Who is trapped upstairs?
   (c) How will she be rescued?
   (d) What are the ambulance men doing?
   (e) Why is the dog barking?

3 Write questions which would give these
   answers. Remember the question mark.
   (a) There were three people in the house.
   (b) They didn't have any pets.
   (c) No, the fire hasn't spread to another house.
   (d) I don't know what caused the fire.
   (e) Yes, I know the people who live there.

B. Word puzzle

All the vowels have been left out of these words. Try to read them.
Write them and put in the missing vowels.

l–dd–r   p–l–c–   c–r

f–r–m–n   w–t–r   h–s–   h–lm–t

–mb–l–nc–   w–ll–ngt–ns

When you have finished, look up the words in a dictionary to make sure you have spelt them correctly.

C. Write a letter.

Pretend that one of your friends lived in the house where the fire broke out He or she has been taken to hospital.

Write a letter saying how sorry you are and that you hope your friend will be home soon. Give any news you can.

Set out your letter like this.

>   27 Birch Terrace,
>   Newtown.
>   27 September.
>
>   Dear Chris,
>   I am very sorry....
>
>
>
>
>
>
>   Your friend,
>   Pat

D. Make a fire frieze.

You will need

paper to draw on

pencil

black frieze paper

paints or crayons

thin card

adhesive and pasters.

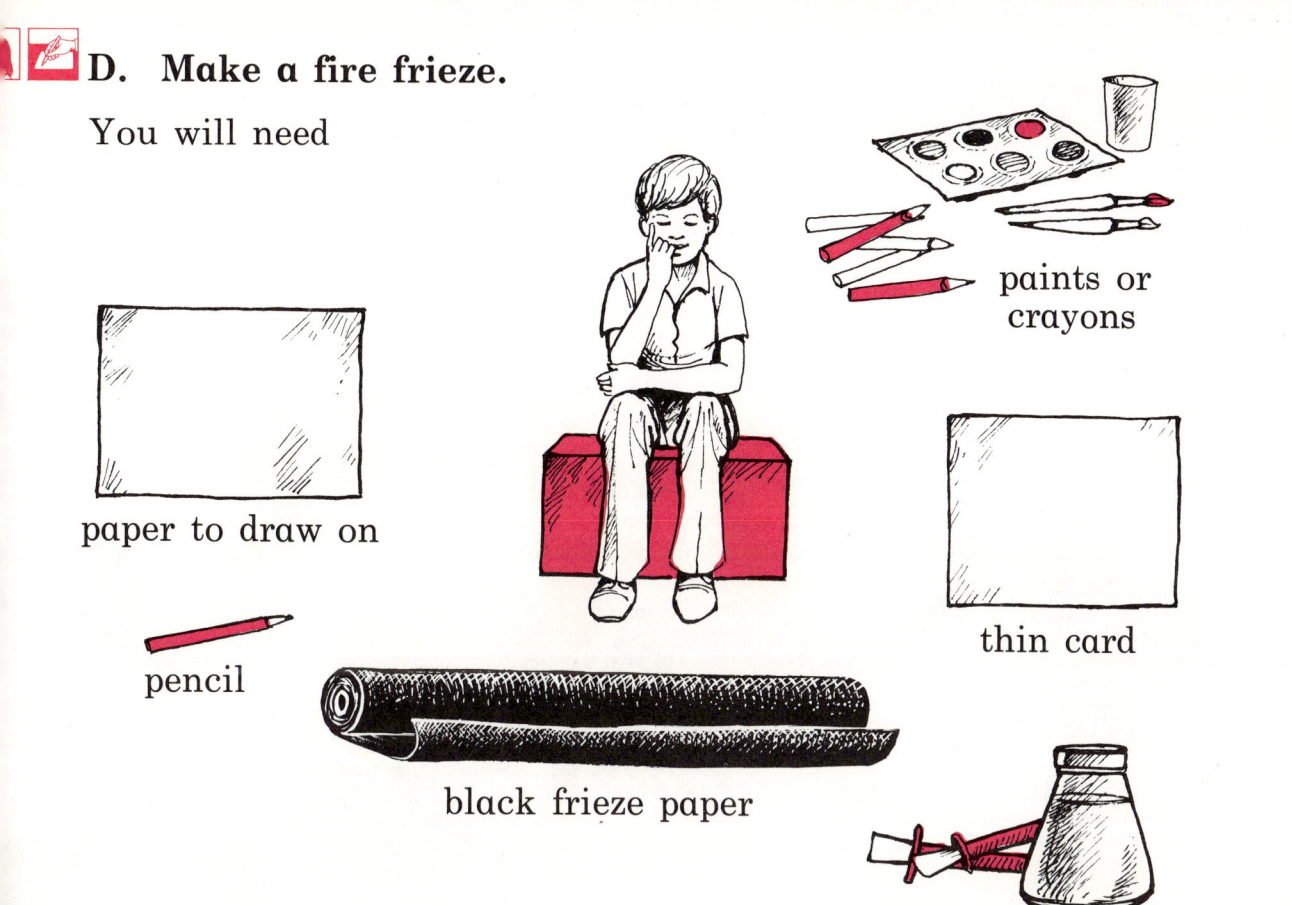

Divide into 4 groups.

Group 1
Make pictures of houses for a street.

Group 2
Make pictures of men, women and children.

Group 3
Make pictures of firemen, policemen and ambulance men.

Group 4
Make pictures of fire-engines, police cars and ambulances.

Arrange the finished pictures on the black paper to show a street. When you have a good arrangement, paste the pictures on to the black frieze paper.

Write on pieces of card what you think people are saying. Paste them on at suitable places.

UNIT 11

A. Talk about the picture.

1. What season of the year does this picture show?
2. What are the children doing?
3. Do you think they are enjoying themselves? How do you know?
4. What do you like to do on a snowy day?

B. Make a poem.

1. Write four words which describe the picture above. (white, sparkling, ____, ____)
2. Write the names of four things or people in the picture. (children, sledge, ____, ____)
3. Write four words which describe the children. (happy, young, ____, ____)
4. Make a five-line poem like the one below. Write the word "Snow" in the first and last line. Choose two words from your list 1, three words from your list 2, two words from your list 3.

Snow
white   sparkling
children   sledge   snowball
young   happy
Snow

C. **Talk about the picture.**

1 What season of the year does this picture show?
2 What is the difference between this picture and the one on page 38?
3 What do you think will happen to the travellers?
4 How would you feel if you were one of the travellers?

D. **Make a poem.**

1 Write four words which describe the picture above. (wintry, frightening, ____, ____)
2 Write the names of four things or people in the picture. (cars, travellers, ____, ____)
3 Write four words which describe the travellers. (freezing, worried, ____, ____)
4 Make a poem in the same way as you did on the opposite page. This time use words from your new lists for lines 2, 3 and 4.
5 Draw a picture for each of your poems. Make a wall frieze with the pictures and poems.

E. Read your poem.

Take it in turn to read your poem to the class or group, or record it on tape for others to hear.

If you listen to recorded poems, can you say who is speaking?

F. Describing words

Copy into your workbook the describing words in the left-hand box.

After each describing word write a suitable noun from the right-hand box.

Begin like this: *huge snowball*

happy trapped	snowball children
icy	wind
huge wooden	cars sledge

G. Sentences

Write these as correct sentences, putting in capital letters, full stops or question marks.

1 susan and peter made a great big snowball
2 do you like playing in the snow
3 it was wednesday before they got away

A. **Book titles**

1 What is meant by the title of a book?
2 What would you expect to read in each of these books?

50 Tasty Supper Snacks

Key Maths

Murder at Midnight

Tales for Toddlers

Tunes for the Recorder

Verses for Children

UNIT 12

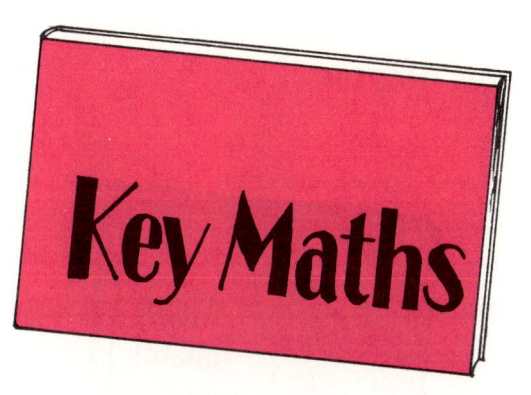

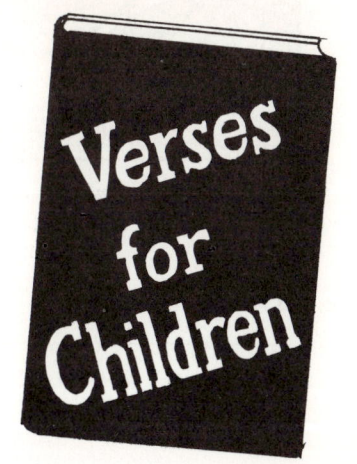

B. **Capital letters**

The first word of a title and all its main words begin with a capital letter.

Write these book titles, putting capital letters where they should be:

1 black beauty
2 stig of the dump
3 the little house on the prairie
4 a gift from winklesea
5 charlie and the glass elevator

C. Choosing a book

In bookshops and libraries you will find many different kinds of books. Here is a list of some, and 10 picture covers. Choose the correct picture cover to go with each kind of book and write the title. The first one has been done for you.

1   Monster story *The Thing from the Deep*
2   Ghost story
3   Adventure
4   History
5   Animal story
6   Superhero
7   Space adventure
8   Funny story
9   Police story
10 Fairy tale

D. a or an

> *Remember* a before a consonant
> an before a vowel

Put **a** or **an** correctly in the spaces.

1   *The Thing from the Deep* is _____ exciting story.
2   *Black Bess* is the story of _____ horse.
3   I read _____ interesting poem.
4   The library has _____ good selection of books.
5   *Dial 999* has _____ unusual ending.

E. Nouns (naming words)

Write the 7 nouns (naming words) from these 3 titles.

1 The Dog and the Bone
2 The Lion, the Witch and the Wardrobe
3 The Sword in the Tree

F. Find out.

Find out the names of five authors.
Write the title of at least one book each author has written.

G. Reading aloud

Take it in turn to read to your group a small part of a book you have enjoyed.

H. Extra

Draw a cover for two of the books in this list.

1 Lost in the Hills
2 Storm at Sea
3 The House with Five Chimneys
4 Ballet Dancer
5 Freddie, the Football Fan

A. Limericks

UNIT 13

    There was a young boy from Brazil
    Who swallowed a nuclear pill.
    He first went bionic
    And then supersonic,
    And now he is dangerously ill.

This verse is called a limerick.
Limericks are funny poems.
They have five lines.
Many limericks start "There was a _____" or
"There once was a _____".
The words at the end of lines 1, 2 and 5 rhyme.
The words at the end of lines 3 and 4 rhyme.

1 Write the next limerick. Choose suitable words from this list to fill in the spaces.

    blue do sight fright

    There was a young girl from Peru
    Whose hair turned an odd shade of _____.
    She called out in _____
    "I'm a terrible _____
    And I really don't know what to _____."

2 In the next limerick the lines are written in the wrong order. Rewrite the lines neatly, and put them in the correct order.

    Who played the guitar all day long.
    The neighbours protested,
    And that was the end of the song.
    There once was a girl from Hong Kong
    And had her arrested,

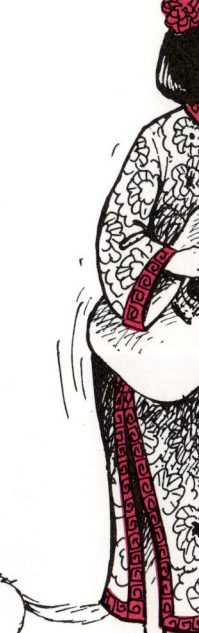

B. Spelling and meaning

Did you notice that in the limericks on page 45 the rhyming words did not always have the same spelling for the rhyming part?

Peru   blue   do

Sometimes whole words sound exactly alike but have a different spelling and a different meaning.

1 Read these pairs of words:

night, knight   here, hear   son, sun
sum, some   nose, knows

Talk with your group and teacher about the meanings of each pair of words and then do Exercise 2.

2 Choose the correct word from the brackets. Write each sentence.

(a) The $\begin{pmatrix} \text{night} \\ \text{knight} \end{pmatrix}$ rode on horseback.

(b) He $\begin{pmatrix} \text{nose} \\ \text{knows} \end{pmatrix}$ all the answers.

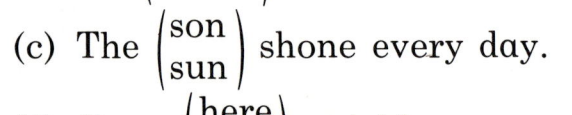

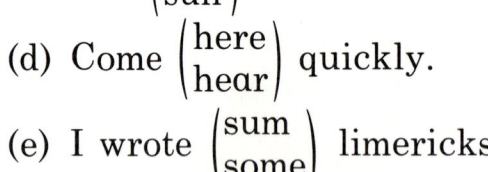

(c) The $\begin{pmatrix} \text{son} \\ \text{sun} \end{pmatrix}$ shone every day.

(d) Come $\begin{pmatrix} \text{here} \\ \text{hear} \end{pmatrix}$ quickly.

(e) I wrote $\begin{pmatrix} \text{sum} \\ \text{some} \end{pmatrix}$ limericks.

C. Kim's Game

1 Look for a short time at the things on the tray. Close your book and write as many of the things as you can remember.

2 You can play this game with your group, using things from the classroom. One person from the group should choose the things to put on the tray.

3 You can play this game with words instead of things.

Look at the words for a short time and try to remember them. Now close your book and write all the words you remember.
How many words did you write?
How many did you spell correctly?
Check carefully.

D. The nose knows!

Here are eight words. Find other words that sound exactly the same but have a different spelling. The first two have been done for you.

1 knows *nose*   3 their   5 sore   7 stake
2 by *buy*   4 blue   6 rode   8 eye

E. Answer the questions.

Here are three questions about the limericks on page 45. Answer in sentences.

1 What made the boy from Brazil unwell?
2 Where did the girl who played the guitar live?
3 Why was the lady from Peru upset?

Check your sentences.

F. Who is it?

1 Describe the child in the picture.
2 Divide into groups. Take it in turn to describe another person in your group. Who can guess correctly?

G. Extra

1 Draw a picture to go with one of the limericks on page 45.
2 Try to make up a limerick of your own.

Checkpoint 2

1   Write these words in alphabetical order.

   (a)   zero mask knock yacht empty

   (b)   sort spoon scratch sack stick

2   Write the nouns (naming words) from each sentence.

   (a) The girl played a tune on the piano.
   (b) The lady bought apples, pears and bananas.
   (c) The boy visited the dentist.

3   Write the verbs (doing words) from this sentence:

   The man wrote a letter, addressed the envelope, stamped it and posted it.

4   Write a describing word to go with each noun.

   (a) woollen   gloves
   (b)   pencil
   (c)   story
   (d)   dress
   (e)   witch
   (f)   potato

5   Complete these sentences:

   (a) The day before Wednesday is _____.
   (b) _____ is the day after Saturday.
   (c) Tomorrow is _____.
   (d) Yesterday was _____.

6   Write the questions which would give these answers:

   (a) Yes, I have a sister.
   (b) The shop opens at two o'clock.
   (c) I am eight years old.

UNIT 14

7 The vowels are missing from these words. Write the whole word. You can use all these things to go from place to place.

   (a) c–r   (b) l–rr–   (c) tr– –n
   (d) h–l–c–pt–r   (e) b– –t   (f) b–c–cl–

8 Write:
   (a) the title of this book
   (b) the name of the author.

9 Write (a), (b) and (c) as correct sentences, putting capital letters, question marks and full stops in the right places.

   (a) when will my present arrive
   (b) i read a story called pippi longstocking
   (c) on tuesday we are going swimming with our friends moira and tom

A. Read the story, then make up 6 questions about it.
Write the questions in your workbook.
Remember the capital letter at the beginning and the question mark at the end.

Mrs Pepperpot at the Airport

The day came and Mrs Pepperpot took the bus to the airport. It was quite a long trip and the other passengers were a bit surprised to see her get on in her old-fashioned clothes and carrying a broom.

At the airport there was a great crowd of people, and they stared even more at the little old woman with her shawl and her broom. Some of them were talking in foreign languages, and everyone was carrying heavy suitcases and pushing this way and that. By the time the loudspeaker announced that the plane from New York was about to land, Mrs Pepperpot was so confused, she didn't know if she was standing on her head or her heels. As it happened, it didn't matter very much, because at that moment she shrank.

From *Mrs Pepperpot's Outing*
by Alf Prøysen

UNIT 15

B. Nouns and verbs

Pretend you are going on holiday. Write the names of five things you would take with you. (Naming words are nouns.) Write five verbs which tell what you would like to do on your holiday. (Doing words are verbs.)

C. Describing words

Write out these sentences, putting a describing word in the spaces. You will find all the describing words for the spaces in the Mrs Pepperpot story on page 51.

(a) It was quite a _____ trip.
(b) Mrs Pepperpot wore _____ clothes.
(c) The people at the airport stared at the _____ woman.
(d) Everyone was carrying _____ suitcases.
(e) Some people were talking in _____ languages.

D. Sentences

Write out these sentences, putting capital letters, full stops and question marks in the right places.
(a) we are flying to america
(b) have you ever been there
(c) our plane leaves on tuesday
(d) how long are you staying

E. Write a letter.

Write a letter to a friend telling about a holiday. Say what you have been doing. Remember to set out your letter like the one on page 36. Write your address and the date clearly.

F. Missing words

1 Some words have been missed out of this story. What do you think they are? Write out the story, putting the missing words in the spaces.

Alan got into his car and drove off at great speed. His plane would leave in fifteen _____ and if he did not reach _____ airport in time he would have _____ wait till the next day. After _____ had been driving for a very _____ time he was stopped by a _____ car. There was now no hope _____ meeting his friend at the time _____ had arranged.

2 Talk with your group and teacher about the words which were chosen.

G. Extra

To pass the time on a journey it is nice to have something to do. Here is a crossword to try.

Draw the crossword square in your workbook.

Clues

Across
1 We swim in it.
3 Used for fishing.

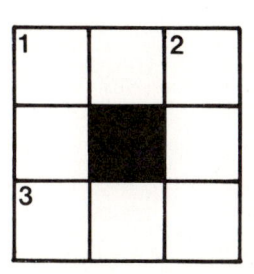

Down
1 It gives heat.
2 An insect.

UNIT 16

Which is the winner?

Look at this picture of a race. Each boat has one of these numbers on the sail:

one   two   three   four   five
six   seven   eight   nine   ten

There are 10 boats in the race, but if we want to tell the **place** of a boat in the race, we say that it is in

first, second, third, fourth,
fifth, sixth, seventh, eighth,
ninth or tenth place.

You can see from the picture that boat number 5 is in first place, and boat number 8 is eighth.

A. **Write answers to these questions.**

1 What places do the following boats take?
 (a) 10   (b) 4   (c) 7   (d) 1   (e) 8

2 Draw a picture of the boat in each of these places:
 (a) fifth   (b) sixth
 (c) ninth   (d) second

B. Make a picture.

1. Read this description of a ship called the *Dawn Treader*.
2. Look in the dictionary for the meaning of any words you don't know. Write these words.
3. Make a coloured picture of the ship.

Her prow was gilded and shaped like the head of a dragon with wide open mouth. She had only one mast and one large, square sail which was a rich purple. The sides of the ship – what you could see of them where the gilded wings of the dragon ended – were green. She had just run up to the top of one glorious blue wave, and the nearer slope of that wave came towards you, with streaks and bubbles on it.

From *The Voyage of the Dawn Treader*
by C. S. Lewis

C. Describing words

Write a describing word for each noun.

describing word	noun
(a)	sea
(b)	island
(c)	treasure
(d)	voyage
(e)	cliffs

D. Maps

This is a map of a group of islands. Look at it carefully and use it to answer these questions.

(a) What is the name given to this group of islands?
(b) What is the name of the smallest island?
(c) What is the name of the biggest island?
(d) On which island is Bernstead?
(e) On which island is Narrowhaven?
(f) What does an island have all round it?

E. Write a story.

Write a story about a voyage to Narrowhaven. Start with these two sentences:

In the morning we set sail towards Narrowhaven. The sea was calm and the sky was blue.

What happened next? Perhaps a storm arose. Perhaps pirates attacked your ship. Perhaps you sailed to a treasure island. Did you ever get to Narrowhaven?

UNIT 17

A. Machines

1. Look at this picture.
   - (a) What is it?
   - (b) How is it used?
   - (c) Do you think it is useful? Give reasons.

2. After you have collected your shopping in a supermarket, a machine shows how much you have to pay.
   How is the machine used?
   Is this a good thing? Give reasons.

B. Your senses

You feed the machines on page 58 with information and they give back information. The same thing happens with your brain. It takes in information through 5 senses:

seeing   hearing   touching   tasting   smelling

These 5 senses send messages to your brain. Your brain replies to the messages.

1 Look at these pictures.
   (a) Which sense is sending a message to your brain?
   (b) What does your brain reply?

2 Your senses not only send warning messages to your brain, they help you to enjoy things too.
Write at least two things you enjoy –
(a) seeing
(b) hearing
(c) touching
(d) tasting
(e) smelling.

C. Describing words

A packet of crisps is needed for this exercise. Each person in the class or group should have one crisp.

1 Look at your crisp.
   Write at least two words which describe it.
2 Snap your crisp into two pieces. Eat one piece. Listen to the sound as you eat it. Write as many words as you can to describe the sound.
3 How does it taste? Write as many words as you can to describe the taste.
4 Touch the part you have left. How does it feel? Write as many words as you can to describe the feeling.
5 Smell the crisp. Write as many words as you can to describe the smell.

Describing words are called adjectives.

D. Missing adjectives

1 Some **adjectives** have been missed out of this story. What do you think they are? Write out the story, putting the missing **adjectives** in the spaces.

It was a _____ day so we packed a _____ basket and set off for the beach.
   We took _____ sandwiches, _____ cake and _____ biscuits. We also took a bottle of _____ juice.
   First we played on the sand with our _____ ball. Next we went for a swim. After that we ate and drank all the _____ things we had brought. What a _____ day it had been!

2 When everyone in your group has finished, talk about the words that were chosen.

E. Singular and plural nouns

We say a noun is **singular** if we are talking about only one.

The **boy** sailed his **boat**.

Boy and **boat** are singular nouns.
We say a noun is **plural** if we are talking about more than one.

The **boys** sailed their **boats**.

Boys and **boats** are plural nouns.
In these words, **s** has been added to the singular noun to make it a plural noun.
Make all the singular words below into plural words by adding **s**. Write them.

   basket   cake   bat   day   bottle

61

UNIT 18

Checkpoint 3

1 Write these words in alphabetical order:

   boy girl husband wife lady
  gentleman woman

2 Write 2 sentences, one to answer each question:

   What is your name?
  Where do you live?

3 The vowels are missing from these words. Write each complete word.

   (a) f--tb-ll   (d) S-t-rd-y
  (b) Sc-tl-nd   (e) P-dd-ngt-n
  (c) l-br-ry   (f) sch--l

4 These 4 sentences tell a story, but they are in the wrong order. Write them out so that they tell the story.

   The glass was shattered.
  One boy kicked the ball into a garden.
  Some boys were playing football.
  The ball struck a greenhouse.

5 Put **a** or **an** correctly before these words.
  umbrella biscuit oil-rig necklace aeroplane

6 Write out each sentence, putting a suitable verb in the space.

 (a) The boy _____ his lunch.
 (b) The children _____ television.
 (c) The gardener _____ his flowers.

7 Write an adjective to go with each noun. Remember, an adjective is a describing word.

adjective	noun
(a)	cake
(b)	pullover
(c)	weather
(d)	bag
(e)	chair

8 Choose the correct word. Write the whole sentence.

 (a) I have (too, two) ears.
 (b) Where did you (buy, by) your coat?
 (c) I went for a (sail, sale) in a boat.

9 On the right is a part of the contents of a reference book. In which sections would you look to find information on each of these?

 (a) canoes   (b) bread   (c) sandals
 (d) elephant   (e) anorak   (f) labrador

Contents

Dogs	5
Wild Animals	25
Wild Flowers	45
The Story of Shoes	70
Clothes	85
Boats and Ships	110
Our Towns	130
What we eat	155

10 Write these as correct sentences, putting in capital letters, full stops and question marks.

 (a) have you read a book called black beauty
 (b) it is the story of a horse
 (c) the author is anna sewell

11 Write the second, fifth, seventh and ninth
   words from the sentence in the box.

   > **We had fried fish and chips for dinner today.**

12 Write a sentence for each picture to show
   what is happening. The first one has been
   done for you.

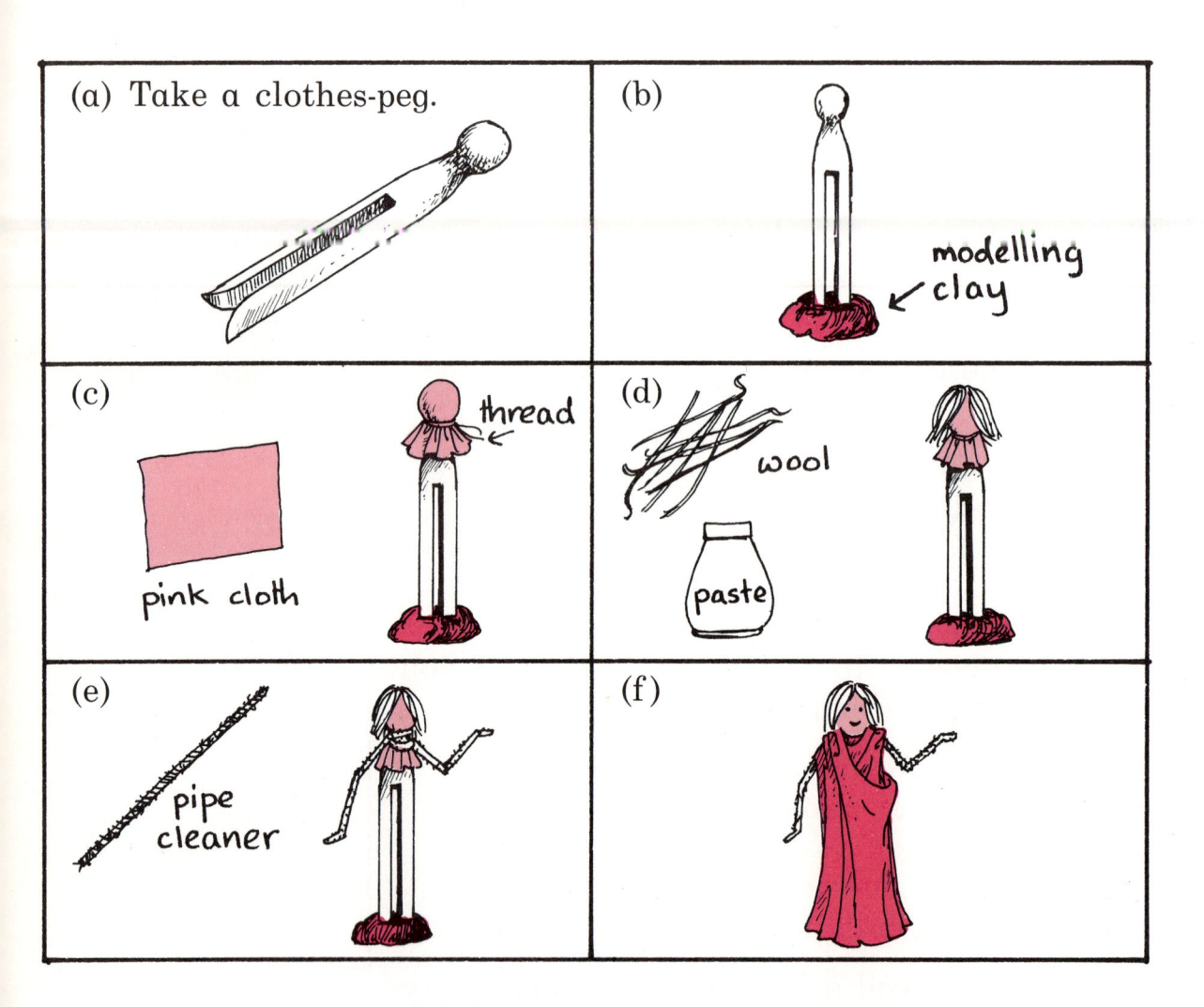

(a) Take a clothes-peg.	(b) modelling clay
(c) pink cloth / thread	(d) wool / paste
(e) pipe cleaner	(f)

13 Make a list of all the things you would need
   if you were going to make this figure.

   Extra
   Make the doll.